Zoom in on
CLIMATE MAPS

Enslow Publishing
101 W. 23rd Street
Suite 240
New York, NY 10011
USA

enslow.com

E

Kathy Furgang

WORDS TO KNOW

climate The kind of weather a certain area has over time.

compass rose A drawing on a map that shows directions.

equator An imaginary line around Earth that separates it into two parts—northern and southern.

hemisphere One half of Earth or another sphere.

humidity The amount of moisture, or water, in the air.

legend A box on a map that explains what the figures on the map mean.

microclimate The climate in a small area.

representation A picture or symbol that stands for, or represents, something else.

zone An area.

CONTENTS

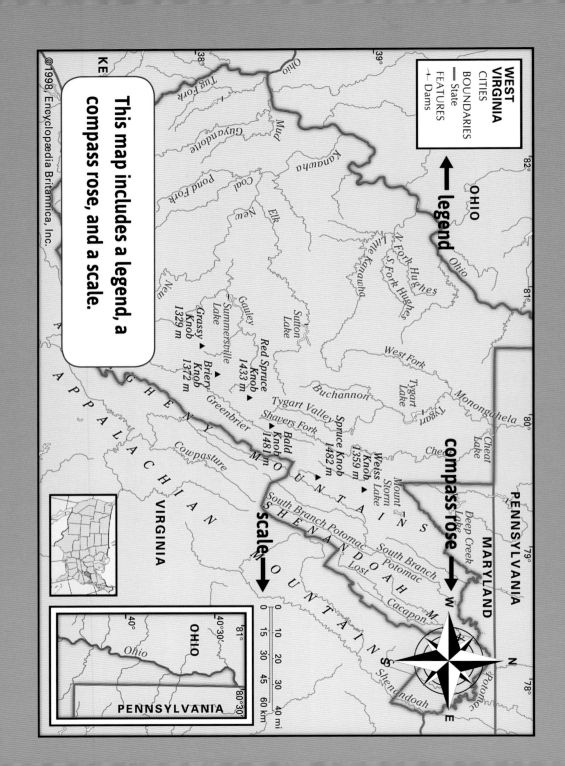

This map includes a legend, a compass rose, and a scale.

WEST VIRGINIA

KEY

CITIES	
BOUNDARIES	
—	State
FEATURES	
⊢	Dams

legend

compass rose

scale

© 1998, Encyclopædia Britannica, Inc.

OHIO

PENNSYLVANIA

MARYLAND

VIRGINIA

APPALACHIAN

ALLEGHENY MOUNTAINS

SHENANDOAH MOUNTAINS

Grassy Knob 1329 m
Briery Knob 1372 m
Red Spruce Knob 1433 m
Bald Knob 1481 m
Spruce Knob 1482 m
Weiss Knob 1359 m

Ohio
Tug Fork
Guyandotte
Mud
Kanawha
Coal
Pond Fork
New
Elk
Little Kanawha
N. Fork Hughes
S. Fork Hughes
West Fork
Tygart Lake
Monongahela
Cheat Lake
Deep Creek Lake
Tygart
Cheat
Buchannon
Tygart Valley
Shavers Fork
Gauley
Summersville Lake
Greenbrier
Cowpasture
Sutton Lake
Red Spruce
Mount Storm Lake
South Branch Potomac
South Branch Potomac
Lost
Cacapon
Potomac
Shenandoah

OHIO

Ohio
PENNSYLVANIA

0 15 30 45 60 km
0 10 20 30 40 mi

N S E W

Maps and Climate

Maps are representations of places. There are many different kinds of maps. Some show natural features of an area, such as rivers, mountains, and deserts. Others show human-made features, like cities, roads, and borders. Maps may show towns, states, countries, or even the world.

Most maps have a few things in common. They all show information using symbols. The legend on a map will explain these symbols to you. Maps also use a compass rose to explain

Predicting the Weather

Knowing the climate of an area can help us figure out what kind of weather to expect there in the future. If the average yearly snowfall in Minnesota is about 32 inches (81 cm), we can expect it to snow there about that much each year.

the four main directions: north, south, east, and west. This book will teach you how to read and understand climate maps.

What Is Climate?

Have you ever wondered what the difference is between weather and climate? Weather is what is happening in the air at any given time. Weather can be rainy, snowy, cloudy, windy, or sunny. Climate is the weather of an area over time. How

are weather and climate related? When people talk about the weather, they usually mean what will happen the next day or the next week. Weather changes all the time. When people talk about the average weather over a longer period of time, they are talking about climate.

The climate of an area is its weather over time. Some areas have hot summers and cold winters, while others have a more steady climate.

Understanding Climate Maps

The climate for an area can be easily shown on a climate map. Climate maps usually show one type of weather. For example, a climate map might show the amount of precipitation that an area gets. Precipitation is any moisture, or water, that falls from the clouds. Rain, snow, and sleet are all types of precipitation. Other climate maps might show the types of precipitation. Temperature maps and precipitation

Climate maps are made by collecting years of weather information. In this map, the yearly snowfall in the United States is shown. Then the mean, or average, is placed on the map.

MEAN ANNUAL SNOWFALL

Adapted from a 1:10,000,000-scale map by
Environmental Data Service, Environmental Science Services Administration
for the period 1931 - 1952

Albers Equal Area Projection

SCALE 1:17,000,000

INCHES	TOTAL	CENTIMETERS
256		650.2
128		325.1
96		243.8
64		182.6
32		81.3
16		40.6
8		20.3
0		0

ALASKA
SCALE 1:38,500,000

No snowfall except on highest peaks

Principal Islands of
HAWAII
SCALE 1:17,000,000

maps are two of the most common kinds of climate maps. Climate maps can show other weather features, such as wind speed or amount of sunshine. They may also show the humidity of an area, which is the amount of moisture in the air.

Be a Legend

It is important to understand the symbols used on a map's legend. On a climate map, the legend explains the colors and symbols used on the map. Look at the climate map on the next page. It shows the average rainfall across the United States in 2015.

Climate and Crops

Farmers often use climate maps to find out what kinds of seeds can be planted in different areas. Different plants grow best in different kinds of weather.

Understanding Climate Maps

Look at the
legend to the
right of the map.
It tells you how
much rainfall
(in inches) the
different colors
represent. For
example, areas
in red or purple
received more rainfall than areas shaded in green or
yellow. Overall, what does this map tell you about average
rainfall in the different parts of the country?

October 01, 2015 Water Year (Oct. 1) Observed Precipitation
Created on: May 10, 2017 - 00:25 UTC
Valid on: October 01, 2015 12:00 UTC

Inches

100
80
70
60
50
40
35
30
25
20
15
10
5.0
2.5
.01

Mapping the Climate

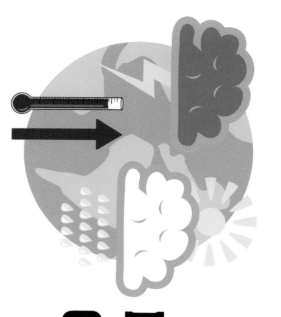

Many maps include imaginary lines. These lines are used to divide the world into different sections. One important imaginary line is called the equator. The equator separates Earth into two halves, called hemispheres. The areas near the equator are the warmest in the world. The areas farthest from the equator are the coldest parts of Earth.

The amount of sunlight in an area has an effect on its climate. As Earth circles the sun, different areas get different

Mapping the Climate

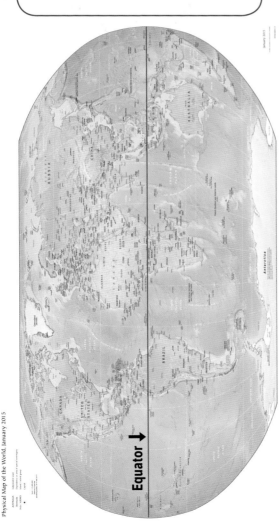

Physical Map of the World, January 2015

Equator →

This map shows the Northern Hemisphere and the Southern Hemisphere, which are divided by the equator.

amounts of sunlight. This is why we have seasons. You can see the effect that the seasons have on climate if you look at climate maps of the same area from different times of the year.

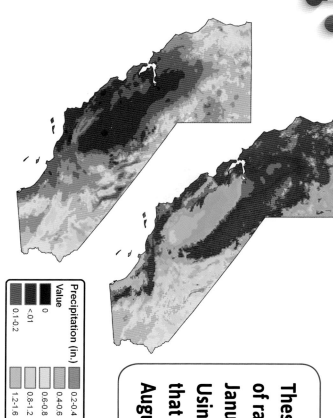

These maps show the amount of rainfall in California in January (top) and August. Using the legend, you can see that the state is much drier in August than it is in January.

Precipitation (in.)

Value					
0	0.1-0.2	0.2-0.4	1.6-2.0	4-5	16-20
<.01		0.4-0.6	2.0-2.4	5-6	20+
		0.6-0.8	2.4-2.8	6-8	
		0.8-1.2	2.8-3.2	8-12	
		1.2-1.6	3.2-4.0	12-16	

Temperature Maps

Temperature climate maps tell us how warm or cool an area usually is. Some temperature maps show the average temperature for a year. Others may show a certain time of year, such as a season or a month.

Precipitation Maps

A precipitation map shows how much and what kind of precipitation is common in an area. Precipitation maps

Cold Climates

The climates on Earth affect where people live. Very few people can live in the most northern areas on Earth because they are bitterly cold year-round.

can show the average amount of one type of precipitation. They can also show the average amount of precipitation for a season or month, or the average number of days of precipitation per year.

In the Zone

There are five major climate zones on Earth. These zones group climates by average temperature and precipitation. They are tropical, dry, temperate, cold, and polar.

A tropical climate, such as that in Hawaii, is warm and wet. A dry climate, such as that in Arizona, is usually warm and without much rain. A temperate climate, such as Ohio, has warm summers and mild winters. A cold climate, such

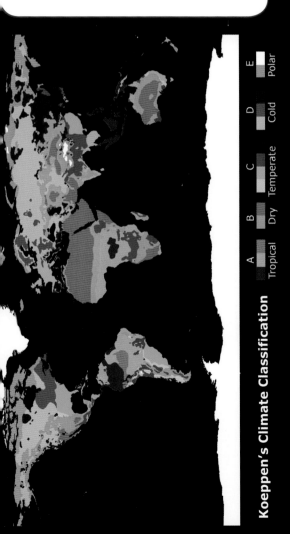

This map shows smaller areas inside each of Earth's five climate zones. The smaller areas show the precipitation for that area.

Koeppen's Climate Classification

A	B	C	D	E
Tropical	Dry	Temperate	Cold	Polar

as Alaska, has warm summers and cold winters. Polar climates are cold year-round. They can be found near the North Pole and South Pole.

Microclimates

A climate map usually looks at a large area. We can also look at the climate of a smaller area, or a microclimate.

When you look at a map that shows microclimates, you can see where the climate changes a lot between two neighboring areas. Many natural features, such as mountains and oceans, can create microclimates. The state of Washington has one of the highest average yearly precipitation amounts in the United States. The Cascade Mountains separate the state into two parts. Rain clouds come off the Pacific Ocean and travel over the state. The mountains act as a wall that keeps the clouds from crossing to the eastern part of the state.

Putting Climate Maps to Use

There are many uses for climate maps. For example, these maps are very helpful for gardeners. Plants need a certain

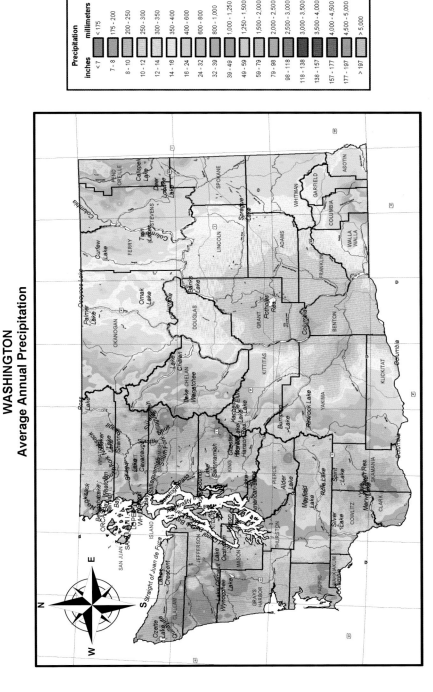

WASHINGTON
Average Annual Precipitation

This map shows Washington State's yearly precipitation. Notice that it rains much more in the state's western part than it does in the eastern part.

kind of weather to grow.
A gardener can use a climate
map to see if it is the right
weather to grow certain plants.
A climate map will show, based
on location, what time of year is
best for planting certain seeds.

Look at the plant hardiness
map on the next page. It shows
the average date of the last frost
in the spring. The companies that sell seeds use maps like
these to show gardeners the best time to plant seeds in
their area.

When to Plant?

A gardener who lives in
Montana would need to
plant her tomatoes later
in the spring than would
a gardener who lives in
Tennessee.

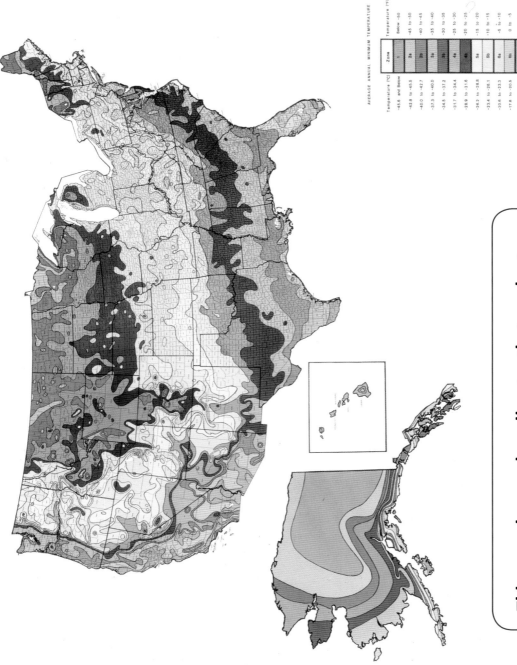

AVERAGE ANNUAL MINIMUM TEMPERATURE

Temperature (°C)	Zone	Temperature (°F)
-45.6 and Below	1	Below -50
-42.8 to -45.5	2a	-45 to -50
-40.0 to -42.7	2b	-40 to -45
-37.3 to -40.0	3a	-35 to -40
-34.5 to -37.2	3b	-30 to -35
-31.7 to -34.4	4a	-25 to -30
-28.9 to -31.6	4b	-20 to -25
-26.2 to -28.8	5a	-15 to -20
-23.4 to -26.1	5b	-10 to -15
-20.6 to -23.3	6a	-5 to -10
-17.8 to -20.5	6b	0 to -5
-15.0 to -17.7	7a	5 to 0
-12.3 to -15.0	7b	10 to 5
-9.5 to -12.2	8a	15 to 10
-6.7 to -9.4	8b	20 to 15
-3.9 to -6.6	9a	25 to 20
-1.2 to -3.8	9b	30 to 25
1.6 to -1.1	10a	35 to 30
4.4 to 1.7	10b	40 to 35
4.5 and Above	11	40 and Above

This map shows microclimates that are best for different plant growth. This research is updated by climate scientists.

ACTIVITY

A TRIP AROUND THE WORLD

Pretend that you are a world traveler. It would help to look at a climate map so that you can plan what to wear. Look at the climate map on page 23. The legend underneath the map tells you what the different colors mean. Use the map to answer each question.

1. Which part of South America has a climate that is most similar to that of the United States?

2. Are you likely to need lighter clothing if you visit Australia or Europe? Why?

3. Which continent has a climate most similar to the climate of North America?

4. On which continents would you need a heavy jacket and gloves?

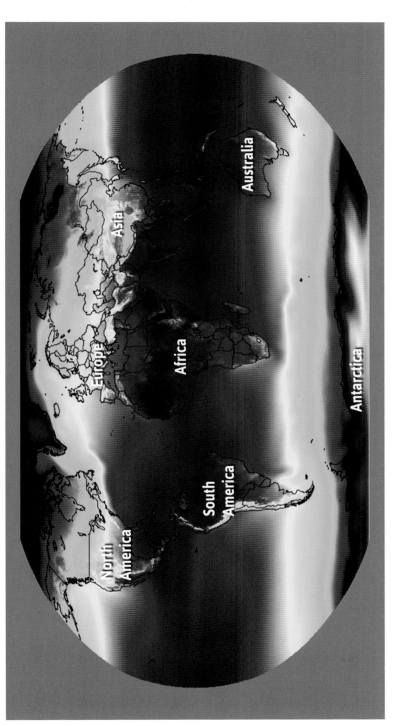

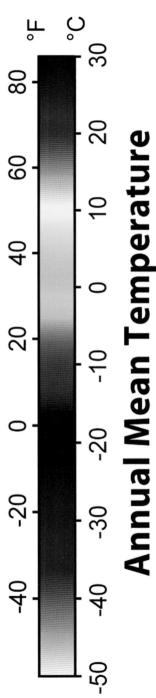

Annual Mean Temperature

LEARN MORE

Books

Hirsch, Rebecca E. *Using Climate Maps.* Minneapolis, MN: Lerner Classroom Books, 2016.

Oabrien, Cynthia. *Climate Maps.* New York, NY: Crabtree Publishing, 2013.

Rajczak, Kristen. *The Climate Zones.* New York, NY: Gareth Stevens Publishing, 2014.

Websites

Easy Science for Kids
easyscienceforkids.com/all-about-climate-around-the-world/
Learn what climate is and why it is important, and read fun facts about climate around the world.

National Geographic Kids Atlas
www.nationalgeographic.com/kids-world-atlas/maps.html
Make your own maps and explore the world by zooming in on maps from around the world.

INDEX

Published in 2018 by Enslow Publishing, LLC.
101 W. 23rd Street, Suite 240, New York, NY 10011

Copyright © 2018 by Enslow Publishing, LLC.
All rights reserved.

No part of this book may be reproduced by any means without the written permission of the publisher.

Library of Congress Cataloging-in-Publication Data
Names: Furgang, Kathy.
Title: Zoom in on climate maps / Kathy Furgang.
Description: New York : Enslow Publishing, 2018 | Series: Zoom in on maps | Includes bibliographical references and index. | Audience: K to Grade 3.
Identifiers: ISBN 9780766092228 (library bound) | ISBN 9780766094284 (pbk.) | ISBN 9780766094291 (6 pack)
Subjects: LCSH: Maps—Juvenile literature. | Weather—Maps—Juvenile literature. Map reading—Juvenile literature.
Classification: LCC GA105.6 F88 2018 | DDC 912.01/4—dc23

To Our Readers: We have done our best to make sure all website addresses in this book were active and appropriate when we went to press. However, the author and the publisher have no control over and assume no liability for the material available on those websites or on any websites they may link to. Any comments or suggestions can be sent by email to customerservice@enslow.com.

Portions of this book originally appeared in *Climate Maps* by Ian F. Mahaney.